AUG 1 3 2009

Using Energy

Sally Hewitt

Crabtree Publishing Company

www.crabtreebooks.com

Crabtree Publishing Company
www.crabtreebooks.com

Author: Sally Hewitt
Editors: Jeremy Smith, Molly Aloian
Proofreaders: Adrianna Morganelli, Crystal Sikkens
Project editor: Robert Walker
Production coordinator: Margaret Amy Salter
Art director: Jonathan Hair
Design: Jason Anscomb
Prepress technician: Katherine Kantor

Activity pages development by Shakespeare Squared
www.shakespearesquared.com

Picture credits: Alamy: pages 8 (bottom), 10, 11, 15, 16-17, 18-19, 22-23, 24-25, 26-27; Druk White Lotus School: page 14; Path to Freedom project: pages 12-13; Ramesh Nibhoria: page 21; Shutterstock: pages 3, 7, 8 (top), 9, 11 (top), 20
We would like to thank Jules Dervaes of the Path to Freedom project for use of his photographs and text relating to solar energy at home.
Every attempt has been made to clear copyright. Should there be any inadvertent omission, please apply to the publisher for rectification.

Library and Archives Canada Cataloguing in Publication

Hewitt, Sally, 1949-
    Using energy / Sally Hewitt.

(Green team)
Includes index.
ISBN 978-0-7787-4096-4 (bound).--ISBN 978-0-7787-4103-9 (pbk.)

    1. Power resources--Juvenile literature. 2. Energy conservation-- Juvenile literature. I. Title. II. Series: Hewitt, Sally, 1949-. Green team.

TJ163.23.H49 2008   j333.79   C2008-903490-2

Library of Congress Cataloging-in-Publication Data

Hewitt, Sally, 1949-
  Using energy / Sally Hewitt.
    p. cm. -- (Green team)
  Includes index.
  ISBN-13: 978-0-7787-4103-9 (pbk. : alk. paper)
  ISBN-10: 0-7787-4103-6 (pbk. : alk. paper)
  ISBN-13: 978-0-7787-4096-4 (reinforced library binding : alk. paper)
  ISBN-10: 0-7787-4096-X (reinforced library binding : alk. paper)
  1. Power resources--Juvenile literature. I. Title. II. Series.

TJ163.23.H49 2008
333.79--dc22

2008023288

Crabtree Publishing Company
www.crabtreebooks.com   1-800-387-7650

Published in Canada
Crabtree Publishing
616 Welland Ave.
St. Catharines, Ontario
L2M 5V6

Published in the United States
Crabtree Publishing
PMB16A
350 Fifth Ave., Suite 3308
New York, NY 10118

Contents

Energy types

Energy is the power to make things work. Food gives us the energy we need to live, grow, and work. Gasoline gives a car energy to move and electricity gives a light bulb energy to glow.

Growing demands

As the number of people living on planet Earth grows year after year, the demand for energy grows, too. There are more and more people using energy for keeping warm or cooling down, for cooking, for turning on lights and machines, and for traveling. The problem to be solved for the future is how to provide enough energy for a growing number of people while looking after the planet, as well.

Challenge!

Write down everything you do that uses these kinds of energy:

- Natural Gas
- Electricity
- Coal
- Wood
- Oil

Think about how much electricity you and your family use every day.

Major cities such as Hong Kong use huge amounts of electricity every day.

Fossil fuels

Fuel is what we burn to make energy. Oil, natural gas, and coal are fossil fuels. They formed from the remains of plants and animals that died millions of years ago. We burn fossil fuels in power stations to make electricity. Gasoline is made from oil so we burn fossil fuels when we ride in a car. This causes the air to become polluted. There is also only a limited amount of fossil fuels left.

Greenhouse gas

As we burn fossil fuels to release energy, smoke from chimneys and exhaust fumes containing a gas called carbon dioxide is released into the air. Carbon dioxide is a greenhouse gas. It helps to trap heat from the sun into Earth's atmosphere and is partly responsible for global warming, which means making Earth warmer.

Saving energy

To be a member of the Green Team, you need to think about saving energy. Saving energy helps to save fossil fuels and may help reduce global warming.

Action!

Choose one thing you can do to save energy.

- Walk to school.
- Turn off the television when you are not watching it.
- Turn lights off in an empty room.
- Get into the habit of doing it every day.
- Now add another action that will save energy.

Global warming is melting ice at the North Pole and South Pole, which causes sea levels to rise. Turtles are threatened by rising seas destroying their nesting beaches.

Coal is burned at this power plant to make electricity. Smoke mixed with greenhouses gases such as carbon dioxide pours into the air, causing pollution and contributing to global warming.

Renewable energy

Energy from natural sources, such as wind, sunlight, and water, is **renewable**, which means it will never run out. It is also clean energy. Fossil fuels do not have to be burned to produce it.

Wind turbines need to be placed where there is plenty of wind. These wind turbines turn in strong sea breezes.

Wind

Wind turns the blades at the top of wind turbines to generate electricity. One turbine on a wind farm can provide clean electricity for 1,000 households per year. Many wind turbines are needed to provide energy for a big city of two million people.

Water

Energy from running water, tides, and waves can be turned into electricity.

Sun

Solar cells in solar panels turn sunlight into energy. Solar panels are used in power plants to provide electricity for a large number of homes.

This solar power plant in Germany is one of the biggest in the world. Its panels turn to follow the sun throughout the day.

Challenge!

Look at all the kinds of natural and renewable energy there are on these pages.

- Find out if any of these kinds of energy are available where you live.

Bio energy

Bio energy is energy stored in plants and animal waste. It is renewable because new plants will grow and animals will make more waste. Biofuel can be burned in power plants. But as it is burned, carbon dioxide escapes into the air. However, biofuel plants take in carbon dioxide as they grow, which helps to reduce the amount of this greenhouse gas in the air.

Geothermal energy

"Geo" means Earth, and "thermal" means heat, so geothermal energy is energy taken from Earth's natural heat. There is very hot, liquid rock called magma under Earth's surface. Heat from magma can be used to make electricity and to heat water and buildings.

 ## Action!

Choose a type of energy on these pages and pages 6-7.

- Write a list of points about it that are good for the planet.
- Write a list of points about it that are bad for the planet.
- Would this type of energy provide enough electricity for everyone who needs it?
- Does any kind of energy have only good points or does any have only bad points?
- Find out about **nuclear energy**, too. What are the good and bad things about this form of power?

Iceland uses natural geothermal energy to generate electricity and heat its homes and buildings. Steam produced by geysers like this one is turned into clean electricity.

Green energy at home

Have you ever thought about where the electricity and gas that powers and heats your home comes from? Is it from power plants that burn fossil fuels, a nuclear power station, or from renewable energy? You can find out, and choose an energy supply that helps to save the planet.

Green supplier

A green electricity supplier will provide electricity from renewable resources— solar, wind, water, or bio energy. Green energy is often a little more expensive but the extra money supports renewable energy and goes toward research and education. The higher prices should help users try harder to save energy at home!

Challenge!

Find out about your energy supplier.

- Is your heating powered by gas or electricity?
- Can you change to a green supplier if you do not already use one?

Every time you turn on a switch, you use energy.

High winds blow over this home in California in winter. The extra electricity generated goes toward saving money on electricity bills.

Wind turbine

A turbine on the roof of a house needs a lot of wind to make enough electricity to power the house. In the right place, it can provide electricity for the home and some to spare. If you live in a windy place, it might be worth having a wind turbine installed on your roof.

Hydropower

Homes near a river or stream may be able to use hydropower. Small water generators, or micro-hydro turbines, can produce enough nonstop energy from running water to power a home.

This river runs all year round creating energy whatever the weather.

Working together

Wind turbines, solar panels, and hydropower systems can be expensive to set up. Groups of people living near each other can join together and apply for a grant or invest in a clean, renewable energy source.

Action!

Make a simple solar oven and use solar energy:

You will need:

large yogurt container
two styrofoam cups
tissue paper
raw carrot sticks
sticky tape
stiff paper
aluminium foil
black paper

1. Line one cup with black paper. Put in the carrot.
2. Cover the sheet of stiff paper with foil, and wrap round the cup to make a cone.
3. Sit the cup in the cone, put this in the other cup, and put in the yogurt container.
4. Stuff tissue paper in the gap between the container and cup to trap heat in.
5. Place the container outside and angle the cone toward the sun. Keep turning to face the sun to cook the carrot.

The foil directs heat from the sun into the container. The black paper soaks up the heat, the tissue paper stops heat escaping, and the carrot cooks in half an hour.

Solar energy at home

Jules Dervaes and his family live in an ordinary house in an average city in southern California. They were worried about the future of the planet because they realized that pollution was harming Earth by causing global warming. So, they asked, "What can we do?"

The solar panels are about three feet (0.9 m) wide and about five feet (1.5 m) long.

Solar panels

The family decided to install twelve solar panels. They were designed to capture light and turn it into clean, renewable energy from the sun, instead of using electricity made from dirty fossil fuels.

Professional help

The first problem was that, although the family wanted to do as much of the work as they could by themselves, they still needed expert help and advice. So, they hired a professional **electrician** to draw up the plans and to help install the panels.

Fitting the panels was slow work at first, until everyone got used to working on the steep, slanted roof.

Challenge!

The Dervaes family live in a sunny place, so solar panels make sense.
Find out what kind of renewable energy would be best for the part of the world where you live.

Fitting the panels

One by one, up went the solar panels. After each panel was bolted in place, the electrical wires were connected to the previous panel. Finally, all the circuits were complete and connected to the main junction box. It was checked by a city inspector and the power was switched on.

The Dervaes family learned that they can do something to help the planet by choosing a clean source of electricity.

After each panel was bolted in place, the electrical wires were connected to the previous panel. Finally, all the circuits were complete and connected to the main junction box.

Mr. Dervaes says:

"We strongly believe that we can change our 'footprint' on this Earth. People can make a difference to bring about a bright and sunny future."

The family was thrilled with the final result.

 Action!

The Dervaes family worked together to change how they use energy.

• Have a family meeting and decide how you can work together to change how you use energy and make a difference.

Your school building

When a new school is built, there is an opportunity to design it as a **sustainable** school. Choosing a renewable energy supply is one of the most important ways a new school can care for the environment.

Case study—Druk White Lotus School in the Himalayas

The Druk White Lotus School is high up in a desert environment where temperatures can drop as low as 8.6° F (-13° C). People built it with locally produced, recyclable materials.
They used both traditional building methods and modern, green design and technology.

Heat and energy

The walls are made of granite with a mud center, a traditional material that **insulates** the building and helps to keep it warm. Electricity is produced by solar power using solar panels.

Sustainable design

Snow cuts off the school in winter, so it is designed to be self-sustainable all year round.
• The school grows its own food in indoor gardens.
• Fresh groundwater is used and recycled.
• Human waste is treated naturally and recycled.

Local building materials, such as stone and wood, help the school to blend in with the natural environment.

No electricity

In many communities around the world, there is either no electricity or very little. This may be good for the planet, but not for schoolchildren. It means they do not have bright lighting for reading and writing and energy to turn on computers, the Internet, or televisions.

Case study—Solar Electric Light Fund (SELF)

SELF is a charity that was set up in 1990 to help bring solar power to rural areas in developing countries. It is running a campaign to bring electricity into schools, called "Brightening lives with solar schools." SELF's new Solar Schools project in South Africa will provide two KwaZulu-Natal high schools with solar energy. This will power lights, TVs, videos, computer labs of 25-30 workstations, Internet access, and links to high-quality distance learning resources.

Action!

Raise money for an organization such as SELF.

These types of organizations install solar or other renewable clean energy in schools in developing countries, giving students the opportunity for a modern education in a sustainable way.

Melusi Zwane, Principal at Myeka High School, one of the schools helped by SELF, says:

"The solar power equipment has had a huge impact on the culture of learning and teaching in our school … The school dropout rate has lowered considerably. You will never understand how much difference the intervention of SELF has made to the education of an African child."

This KwaZulu-Natal high school is powered by solar electricity.

Save energy at home and at school

Making sure electricity is not wasted at home and at school is something that all members of the Green Team can do. By getting into new habits, you can set an example to your parents and teachers.

Sara

Turn off lights when you do not need them but do not leave anyone in the dark!

Turn it off!

The little green, red, or white lights on your television, DVD player, or radio tell you that the machine has been left on **standby** and is using energy and giving out heat. Agree with your parents and teachers what needs to be left on and what can be switched off when it is not in use.

Phone chargers

Leaving a phone charger plugged in and switched on when it is not in use uses electricity and gives out heat. So switch it off and unplug it when your phone is fully charged.

At school

Schools usually spend more money on their electricity bills than they do on books. Cutting back on the amount of electricity used at school not only saves money that can be spent on books instead, but it also helps to look after the planet at the same time.

Challenge!

Spend at least an hour of your free time without turning on a machine.

• Read, play a board or card game, make something, or learn a magic trick instead.

This young student from Teddington, UK, is examining the electronic utilities monitor panel at her school.

A motion sensor turns the lights on when someone is moving in this room, and turns them off when there is no movement.

Case study—An electronic utilities monitor at school

An electronic utilities monitor records power being used and carbon dioxide emissions throughout the day. The Green Team can make a school energy saving plan, put it into action, and check how much energy the school is managing to save. It can also cut its carbon dioxide emissions.

 Action!

Hold an energy week at school. Make a plan of energy saving actions, for example:

- Turn off lights when you leave a room.
- Fit energy-saving light bulbs.
- Shut doors and windows to keep in heat.
- Hold an assembly, invite parents, and tell everyone the plans. Check the school's energy for a week. Compare it with energy use during energy week.

Case study—Oregon

Vale Elementary, Middle, and High Schools in Oregon expect to save nearly three-quarters of their electricity bill by putting in energy-saving light bulbs controlled by motion sensors. This was paid for and organized by Oregon Department of Energy.

Vale School Superintendent, Matt Hawley, says:

"We are more than happy with the results. The new lighting is great. Thanks to the motion sensors, lights get turned off now. Before the project, lights would be turned on for a Saturday morning and they'd stay on all weekend."

Keeping warm

When it is too cold we try to warm up, and when it is too hot we try to cool down. Central heating keeps us warm and air conditioning cools us down. They both use energy. Members of the Green Team look for ways of keeping the correct temperature while also saving energy.

Turn it down! Turn it up!

If you live where it is very cold in winter, you may need to keep the heating on 24 hours a day. If you live where it is very hot, you may have air conditioning to keep you cool. You can save energy by turning the heating down to as low as it is comfortable in the day and even lower at night, and by reducing the air conditioning as much as it is comfortable.

For every degree you turn the heating down or the air conditioning up, you will save money on energy bills!

A **thermostat** keeps the temperature at the setting you choose. Talk about the thermostat setting with an adult. Do not turn it down yourself.

Challenge!

Warm up or cool down without electricity.

- Wear warm clothes in cold weather and have hot drinks.
- Inside, wear a vest, warm socks, and an extra sweater.
- Keep your hands and feet warm.
- Wear cool clothes in hot weather and drink water.
- Make a paper fan to cool you down, not a hand-held battery powered fan

Wearing the right clothes can help to keep you at just the right temperature.

Ask your parents to make sure you have double-glazed windows fitted to keep the heat in.

The red areas show heat escaping from a house.

Escaping air

In winter, warm air escapes from buildings into the cold air outside through cracks and holes and windows, making the heating work harder. There are many ways to fill in the gaps, stop warm air from escaping, and reduce **carbon emissions**.

Keep in the heat!

Adults can:
• Fill in cracks
• Put in double glazing
• Insulate walls and floors
• Keep furniture away from heating vents and radiators

You can:
• Shut doors and windows
• Close curtains at night in the winter

➤ Action!

Make a snake draft excluder.

• You need an old stocking, knee-length sock, or leg warmer longer than the bottom of your door.
• Stuff it with scraps of material so it is evenly filled.
• Tie the end. Give it eyes and a forked tongue.

Carbon offsetting

The aim of **carbon offsetting** is to keep the amount of carbon in the atmosphere the same, and not add to it. The way it is done is by balancing the amount of carbon emissions created by one action with another action that reduces the amount of carbon dioxide in the air.

Airplanes release carbon dioxide high in the atmosphere.

How it works

Step one is to work out how much carbon we put into the air when we do something that uses energy, such as taking a flight to go on vacation.

Step two is to do something that reduces the same amount of carbon in the air, for example, planting a tree or reducing the number of trips we make by car or bus.

Case study— Climate Care

Climate Care is an organization that offsets carbon emissions by funding projects around the world. For example, you can work out the carbon emissions of your family car for a year, and Climate Care will tell you how much offsetting that amount of carbon will cost. They put your money toward a project that uses renewable energy, helps people to reduce their fuel consumption, or replants forests.

Trees take in carbon dioxide in the air and give out oxygen, which we breathe in.

Climate Care Carbon Calculator

- Return flight between New York and London—6,000 miles (9656 km)
- Amount of carbon put into the atmosphere—1.65 tons
- Cost of carbon offsetting—about $23

A worker plants trees in a reforestation area in western Washington.

Nelson Mandela and members of ELI, with one of the company's energy efficient light bulbs.

Climate Care offsetting projects—Reforestation

Cutting down trees means an increase in carbon dioxide as it reduces the number of plants that are able to convert this greenhouse gas into oxygen. Money paid to offset your carbon emissions could go toward replanting forests.

Reducing electricity use

Reducing our use of energy is an important way of reducing carbon emissions, but doing this can be expensive. The Efficient Lighting Initiative (ELI) works in developing countries to promote energy saving.

Most of the electricity in South Africa is made in coal-fired power plants, which have high carbon emissions. To help reduce electricity use, ELI is installing energy efficient lighting where people could not afford it themselves.

Challenge!

Find a carbon calculator on the Internet.

Ask an adult to help you work out the carbon emissions for your family.

Action!

Choose one thing at school that produces carbon emissions and take action.

- Plan ways to reduce the school's use of electricity.
- When you have done this, calculate the carbon emissions and choose how your school would like to offset the emissions.

Transport

Getting around uses energy. When you walk or cycle, you use your own energy. Cars use gasoline and diesel for fuel, airplanes use aviation fuel, and ferries and ships need fuel, too. Members of the Green Team find ways to cut back on burning fuel when they travel.

Traveling by bus rather than by car helps to cut down on carbon emissions.

Heavy traffic in Beijing, China, causes air pollution. It makes people ill and makes global warming worse. People are being encouraged to cycle instead.

Public transport

Traveling by public transport, such as by bus or train, means one big vehicle carrying a lot of people at a time instead of a lot of small vehicles carrying a few people at a time. Fewer vehicles mean less energy is used.

Traveling by bike

Cycling to work or school is the greenest way to travel. Bikes release no greenhouse gases at all.

Challenge!

Choose a journey that you often make by car, for example going to school or to the store.

- Find out how you could get there on public transport.
- Try to do about one in three of those journeys on public transport in the future.

24

Cheap flights make it possible for people to travel around the world on vacations.

Flying

Flying has made the world a smaller place because people can travel around the world quickly and cheaply on vacations and on business. But flying adds to carbon emissions in the air. More and more flights are planned, which will add to the problem.

Going on a vacation

Going on a vacation usually involves traveling by car, boat, train, or plane. You can choose to calculate the carbon emissions of your journey and offset them (see pages 22-23). You can also choose a vacation that does not involve long journeys in vehicles that burn fuel.

 Action!

Plan a vacation week at home for all the family that involves very little travel.

- Do something special every day.
- Go to interesting places nearby, for example a nature reserve or museum.
- Work out how to get there on public transport.
- Plan a circular walk starting and ending at home.
- Pack a picnic and enjoy being outside all day.
- Enjoy your local park, swimming pool, and tennis courts.

This family traveled by bus to get here. They are supporting their local nature reserve and having a good day out.

Going to school

In the morning and in the mid-afternoon, the roads get very busy as children are taken to school and collected by car. Green Team members try to reduce the fuel they burn getting to school by sharing rides, traveling on public transport, the school bus, cycling, or walking.

Cycling to school is a great way to save energy and also to get fit.

Saving energy

To reduce the number of school journeys, some families take turns driving their own children and other children to school. Others encourage their children to walk or cycle to school.

Challenge!

If you cannot ride a bike, learn how to.

- If you do not have a bike, ask if you can borrow a friend's and try it out.
- Encourage your family to cycle with you.
- Wear a helmet and find safe places to ride.
- Take a cycling proficiency course.

Case study—Sustrans Bike It!

Sustrans is short for sustainable transport. This group runs a program called Bike It, which encourages children to cycle to school. A Sustrans Bike It officer works with twelve schools, explaining the benefits of cycling and organizing events and activities to motivate and inspire more children to cycle to school.

Louise, 12, says:

"Bike It is a good thing because it is more refreshing cycling than going in a car. I think it is important to stop pollution further, and cycling helps the environment."

These children are taking a walking bus to school in Hertfordshire, England. They are walking together, forming a human bus.

International Walk to School Month

Case study— Walk to School

International Walk to School month is an annual event to raise worldwide awareness of walking issues. Students everywhere can join in with children all over the world and walk to school for a month.

The walks promote:
- Physical activity
- Road awareness
- Awareness of how walkable a community is and where improvements can be made
- Concern for the environment
- Reducing traffic congestion, pollution, and traffic speed near schools
- Taking back neighborhoods for people on foot

 Action!

Get involved with Walk to School Month and then make walking to school a habit.

Walking buses are used all over the world. Here, children are walking to school on the island of Funafuti in Polynesia.

Wind power!

Harness the power of the wind, a clean and renewable energy source.

Let's Get Started!

Wind power is an excellent way to make electricity without burning fossil fuels. A turbine in a windy area can provide a lot of electricity.

Imagine you were to build a windmill near your home. You would want to place it where it would catch the most wind. The following activity will explain how to find out where the wind blows the most. You will also learn a good way to spread the word about wind as a clean energy source.

Activity

Is your city or town windy enough to make energy? Where do you think the windiest local spot is? To find out, you will need an **anemometer**. An anemometer is a wind-measuring device. Certain government agencies will loan you an anemometer for free. Check with your state's energy administration or with the U.S. Department of Energy for information. Another option is to make your own anemometer. Visit this website to learn how: www.weatherwizkids.com/anemometer.htm

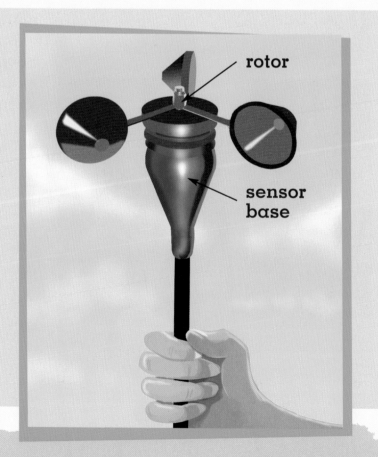

rotor

sensor base

Brainstorm with your class about likely windy locations in your area. Keep in mind that open spaces unobstructed by trees or buildings are often windy. After you think of a list of places, your teacher will assign small groups of students to visit each location. Each group, along with an adult, will take turns after school using the anemometer to measure the wind speed and record the results.

Compare the groups' findings to discover the windiest location. Do you think this would be a good place to install a turbine to generate electricity? How could you get one built?

Looking Back

As a class, write a persuasive letter to the editor of your local newspaper. Suggest that utilizing wind power would be a wise investment. Explain what the benefits of wind power would be to your area. Summarize your experiment and its results. Make sure to explain why this idea is important to you.

To increase the likelihood of your letter being published, follow these guidelines:

Hints for Writing Letters to the Editor

• Follow the newspaper's submission rules. Information about how to submit a letter to the editor can usually be found on the letters page. Or, call the newspaper and ask.

• Keep your letter short and focused. Letters should be no longer than two hundred words. The content should focus on one main point.

• Include your contact information. Sign your names and put your grade, the name of your teacher, and the name of your school on the letter.

Glossary

Carbon emissions
Carbon emissions are the carbon that is sent into the atmosphere when we burn fuels such as coal, oil, and gas for energy.

Carbon offsetting
Carbon offsetting is balancing the amount of carbon put into the atmosphere with an action that reduces carbon in the atmosphere so that the amount of carbon does not increase.

Electrician
An electrician is a person who installs, operates, or repairs electrical equipment.

Energy efficient
To be energy efficient is to use energy in a way that is not wasteful. For example, people can insulate their homes to stop heat from escaping.

Insulate
To insulate a building is to protect it from heat escaping or cold air getting in. For example, people should fill in cracks, and line their homes with insulating material.

Nuclear energy
Nuclear energy is energy released when atoms are split up. Although it is a clean source of energy, it produces dangerous radioactive waste that has to be kept safe for thousands of years.

Renewable energy
Renewable energy is generated from something that can be replaced, such as biofuel from plants, or will never run out, such as wind, water, and sunlight.

Standby
A machine on standby can be turned on by remote control. It is not completely turned off. A small light indicates it is still using energy and producing heat.

Sustainable
Something sustainable can be kept going. Using energy in a sustainable way means using it in a way that does not use it all up or destroy the environment.

Thermostat
A device that senses the temperature and keeps it at a steady level. A thermostat set at about 64° F (18° C) turns the central heating on or off to keep the temperature in the building as near as possible to 64° F (18° C).

Websites

www.iwalktoschool.org/photos
Learn about International Walk to School Month and find out how you can join in with students all over the world and walk to school for a month.

www.sustrans.org.uk
Sustrans—short for sustainable transport— is an organization that gets people to travel in a way that is healthy for them and for the environment.

www.climatecare.org
Climate Care offsets your carbon dioxide by funding renewable energy and energy efficiency projects around the world.

www.self.org
The Solar Electric Light Fund (SELF) is a non-profit charitable organization that promotes, develops, and facilitates solar rural electrification and energy SELF-sufficiency in developing countries.

www.eco-schools.org
Your school can become part of an international group of schools committed to caring for the environment.

www.actionaid.org
Find out about Actionaid's Power Down initiative and how schools can lead the way and be part of the solution to climate change.

Note to parents and teachers:
Every effort has been made by the Publishers to ensure that these websites are suitable for children, that they are of the highest educational value, and that they contain no inappropriate or offensive material. However, because of the nature of the Internet, it is impossible to guarantee that the contents of these sites will not be altered. We strongly advise that Internet access is supervised by a responsible adult.

Index

Printed in China